SEASONS *of*

Aotearoa

New Zealand

Bronwen Wark

Heinemann

PRIMARY

ACKNOWLEDGEMENTS

I would like to thank all the children, parents and staff of the Correspondence School who contributed or assisted in any way, especially the following:

Sally Rawnsley, Ormond Tate, Helen Bissland, the Aldridge family, the Gould family, the Williams family, the Smith family, the Brown family, the Douglass family, the Wark family, the Hook family, the Seon family, the Maher family, the Te Whenua Unit, Ruediger Mack, Judy Southworth, Lyn Davey, Alistair Barr, Bev Webber, Dave Capper, Ruth Robison, Sally Nell, Sally Kidd, Jane Mason, Rick Noesgaard, Tracy Ogden, Zorina Curry, Christopher Belcher, Helen Lee, Michael Gay, Rose Bayliss, Rebecca Kemp Edwards, William Sandbrook, David Hogbin, Lil Urquhart, Brylee Percy, William McKee, Rowena Allen, Sarah Restall.

I would like to thank all the people who were so generous with their time and advice. My special thanks are to the following:

Frank Andrews, George Gibbs, Augy Auer, Stuart Burgess, Floor Anthoni, Bob Drey, Liz Kaiwai, the late Richard Sibson, Phil Sirvid, Grace Hall, Gary Williams, Steve Whitehouse, John Dunlop, John Walsby, Morris Miles, Richard Chesher, Edward Abraham, Dave McLellan, Geoff Moon, Bert McLean, Ronan Browne, Frank Hudson, Maureen Young.

Special thanks to NIWA for supplying the weather statistics, to the Auckland Observatory for permission to reproduce the sky charts on pages 6 and 7, and to Caren Glazer for the diagram on page 8.

PHOTO CREDITS

Introduction
Holger Leue pp 4,5, 6-7

Winter
Holger Leue pp 10,11,12,14,15,16,19,22,23,25
Graham Meadows pp 10,22,24,25
Brian Donovan p 13(x2)
Martin Barriball pp 15(x2),19,25
Stephen Robinson pp 17,21
Geoff Moon pp 17,18(x2),20(x3),21
Kirby Wright (Fotopacific) p 24

Spring
Holger Leue pp 28,31(x2),33,35,38
Graham Meadows pp 26,34,37,39,40(x2),41(x2)
Martin Barriball pp 26,32(x2),33,37
Stephen Robinson p 29
Geoff Moon pp 34,35,36(x2),38(x2),39
Ross Setford (Fotopacific) p 27
Royal Observatory, Edinburgh p 29
Australian Picture Library p 30
David Hallett (Fotopacific) p 35

Summer
Holger Leue pp 45, 48(x2), 57
Graham Meadows pp 42,52,55
Martin Barriball pp 43,47,51,55,56,57
Stephen Robinson pp 44,47,50, 56
Geoff Moon pp 42,50,51,52,53(x3),54
John Dunlop p 45
Ross Land (Fotopacific) p 46,49
Bill Cooper (Fotopacific) p 46
Australian Picture Library p 49
Spencer Currie (Fotopacific) p 54
Fotopress p 47
Mark Walsh (Fotopacific) p 57

Autumn
Holger Leue pp 59,62(x2),65,71
Graham Meadows pp 58,67,71,73
Martin Barriball pp 64,68,69,70
Geoff Moon pp 58,60,66(x2),67,68,69,73
John Dunlop p 61
Rob Suisted p 63
David Hallett (Fotopacific) p 63,71
Brian Moorhead (Fotopacific) p 65,72
John Speller (Fotopacific) p 67

First published 1997 by Heinemann Education, a division of Reed Publishing (NZ) Ltd, 39 Rawene Road, Birkenhead, Auckland. Associated companies, branches and representatives throughout the world.

ISBN 1 86944 193 1

© 1997 Bronwen Wark

Editor: Judith Hodge
Book design by Clair Stutton

Printed by Kings Time Printing Press Ltd, Hong Kong

CONTENTS

PREFACE

OBSERVING and marking the development of the seasons in New Zealand is a wonderful way to learn about the country in which you are living or visiting.

This book aims to encourage people to make their own observations. There are many seasonal 'signposts' to watch out for, such as the birds which live in or visit the country, the happenings in New Zealand's unique native bush and the seasonal changes in the stars of the Southern Hemisphere.

For a fresh perspective on the seasons, we have gathered together the observations of many of the pupils and parents of The Correspondence School. This school is unique in that it has pupils all over New Zealand, many of whom live in isolated places, which made their observations very interesting.

Some of their observations are peculiar to New Zealand, because the flora and fauna are native to this country. Other examples of plants, trees and birds are introduced ones, brought to New Zealand by 19th century European settlers. These species follow the same seasonal patterns as they do in the Northern Hemisphere: the autumn colouring-up and falling of leaves from deciduous trees, for example.

As you read this book, you will discover what children in other parts of New Zealand feel about the seasons, what things they do during the different seasons, and what special signs they have come to associate with a specific season.

INTRODUCTION

THE seasons of the Northern Hemisphere are more clearly defined than New Zealand's seasons. There are parts of the country, however, which do have quite distinctive seasons: places of higher altitude, such as the mountain ranges, and places of lower latitude, like the southernmost part of the South Island.

In other parts of New Zealand, where the climate is temperate, the seasons are still quite different from each other, but these differences are more subtle.

A mountain chain running like a spine down the length of the country also has a significant impact on the climate in different regions. The mountains create a sharper climatic contrast from west to east than from north to south.

People's lives are affected by the seasons. There are many activities, work or leisure, which are influenced and determined by seasonal patterns. Today, with urban expansion, most people do not live so close to the earth. Those who depend on the land or the ocean for their livelihood are often more in tune with the seasons.

Some of the signs of the seasons are welcomed and enjoyed, such as the flowering of the kowhai and pohutukawa trees. Other seasonal occurrences, such as the arrival of wasps and sandflies, are not as well appreciated!

Before European settlement of this country, the Maori people had extensive knowledge and awareness of the different seasonal changes. They needed to observe very carefully the different movements of the sea, the birds and the sky, as well as the flowering and fruiting of the plants and trees, because they lived so close to the earth.

One of the most important seasonal signs for the Maori was the appearance of certain stars in the early morning sky.

The seasonal year for the Maori began around the winter solstice when the star cluster they called Matariki (known to Europeans as Pleiades) first appeared in the eastern morning sky. The first new moon after the appearance of Matariki was the beginning of the new year. In winter, the regenerative cycle of the New Zealand flora begins. Tiny buds can be seen forming in the trees and shrubs.

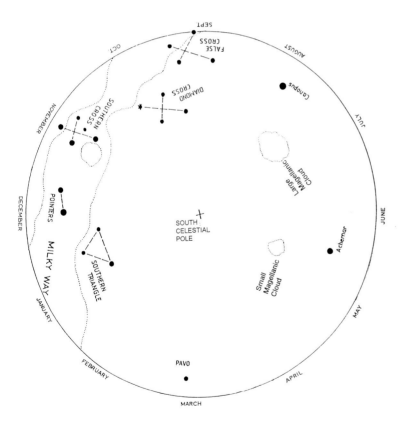

NEW ZEALAND'S BRIGHT CIRCUMPOLAR STARS

These are the stars that are visible in New Zealand's skies every night throughout the year. Their position varies depending on the season.

The Southern Hemisphere sky

PEOPLE visiting New Zealand from the Northern Hemisphere can become quite disorientated if they watch the sky. The sun may appear to be in the 'wrong' part of the sky during the day. At night the moon seems to be rising in the opposite part of the sky than they are accustomed to seeing it, and to be travelling from right to left when they are used to seeing it moving from left to right.

This is because they are used to orientating themselves towards the sun, which in the Northern Hemisphere is in the south. The classical constellations, such as Aries and Taurus, will also appear 'upside down' if the observers are familiar with their position in the northern sky.

The most famous Southern Hemisphere constellation is the Southern Cross, which is also called Crux. The Southern Cross is always accompanied by its pointers, Alpha Centauri and Beta Centauri. It is always in the night sky and can be found in the more southern part of the sky. In the warmer months it will be lower in the south during the early evening, but in the colder months it will be seen higher in the sky at the same time. There are simple bearings which can be taken from the Southern Cross to determine due south.

THE SOUTHERN CROSS

Spring

eta Carina nebula

delta

gamma

CRUX

alpha

beta

Coal Sack

Summer

Winter

omega Centauri

epsilon

beta

POINTERS

alpha

Autumn

What causes the seasons?

THE seasons occur because different places on Earth receive a different amount of sunshine at different times of the year. This is caused by the tilt of the Earth. The axis of the Earth is tilted by 23° with respect to its orbital plane around the sun.

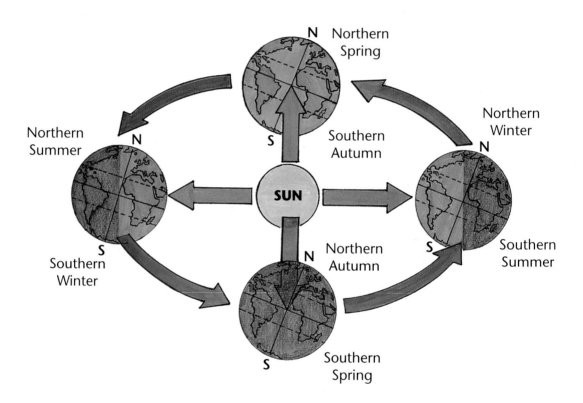

If you think of a ball with a rod through its centre, you can imagine the Earth's axis. The point where the rod enters the ball represents the North Pole, and where it leaves the ball is the South Pole.

When the northern part of the Earth is tilted towards the sun, it is the warm time of year for that part of the globe. This is the season of summer. At the same time, the southern part of the Earth is tilted away from the sun. New Zealand is in this southern part of the Earth, called the Southern Hemisphere. This is our cold time of year, which is the season of winter.

Six months later the situation is reversed. The Southern Hemisphere is tilted towards the sun, so it is summer in New Zealand. The seasons of the two hemispheres are always opposite. So when it is spring in the Northern Hemisphere, it is autumn in the Southern Hemisphere.

The equator is an imaginary line which runs around the middle of the Earth, halfway between the North and South Poles. The equator does not have seasons in the way the Northern and Southern Hemispheres do, because due to its position in relation to the sun, there is light and warmth in this region throughout the year.

The North and South Poles are always cold, but they do have seasons. When it is summer it is light all the time, and when it is winter it is dark around the clock.

Solstices and equinoxes

IN the middle of summer and in the middle of winter, there is a time when the sun is at its furthest point north or its furthest point south. These times are called solstices. In winter the nights are longer than the days, and in summer the days are longer than the nights.

There is also a period, during spring and autumn, which is perfectly 'in-between'. At these times, the days and the nights are of similar lengths. These mid-points of spring and autumn are called the equinoxes (equal nights). An equinox is the halfway point between each solstice. The times of the equinoxes and solstices may vary by a day or two from year to year.

TIMES OF THE SOLSTICES AND EQUINOXES IN NEW ZEALAND
Winter solstice happens between the 20th and 23rd day of June
Spring equinox happens between the 20th and 23rd day of September
Summer solstice happens between the 20th and 23rd day of December
Autumn equinox happens between the 20th and 23rd day of March

WINTER
Takurua, Hotoke

Kohekoh

Some trees are bare,
cold and lonely.
Even birds and
animals are hiding.
The rain falls and
falls.

Rebecca
KAITAIA,
NORTHLAND

I love listening to
the rain on the roof
in winter, because it
sounds neat and it
makes me go to sleep.

Ben
AUCKLAND

WINTER officially begins in New Zealand on the first day of June. The length of night-time is longer than daylight hours during winter.

The winter solstice is between 20 and 23 June. After the winter solstice, when the sun is furthest away from the Southern Hemisphere, New Zealand is slowly turning towards summer, and the days start growing a little longer.

Up until this point, since the last solstice in summer, the days have been slowly getting shorter. Night has been falling earlier, and sunrise coming later each day. The shortest day of the year, which is also the longest night of the year, occurs at the winter solstice.

Temperatures in winter are generally cold. The colder ocean currents from the south move in a northwards direction. The winds are cold, too, and come mostly from the south, bringing all the 'bad' weather of winter: hail, snow, ice and wild storms.

An interesting fact is that the worst of the winter weather always happens quite a few weeks after the winter solstice. This is due to the phenomenon of 'seasonal lag', which is similar to the coldest temperatures of the day occurring one and a half hours after sunrise. The winter 'lag' is about four to six weeks, with the coldest weather occurring from the middle of July through to the middle of August.

Even the north of the country, which is sometimes misnamed 'The Winterless North', experiences colder temperatures. All over New Zealand, winter storms come and go.

The average daily temperatures in winter in the North Island are 15-17°C. In the South Island the average daily temperatures are as low as 3-4°C in some areas of Southland and 12°C in other areas like Nelson.

In winter the snowflakes flutter from the sky like a bird dancing from tree to tree. At night the frost hardens the snow and sometimes you can stand on top of it.

Alana
LAKE TEKAPO,
SOUTH CANTERBURY

The days are very short. We sit by the fire because it is cold. There is no growth.

William
DANNEVIRKE,
HAWKE'S BAY

Location	Rainfall Total (mm) mean monthly	Temperature Mean daily maximum °C	Sunshine Mean hours per day	Relative Humidity Mean daily (%)
Auckland	133	15.1	4.3	86
Napier	84	14.3	4.4	79
Ruapehu	278	6.7	3.0	89
Wellington	139	11.6	3.6	86
Nelson	89	12.6	5.0	89
Christchurch	65	11.8	4.2	87
Dunedin	65	10.5	3.3	80

THE SKY

In winter there are the clear, star watching skies when it is dark by 6 pm. There are lunar eclipses, comets, shooting stars, and the more special Aurora Australis, with its marvellous moving curtains of colour, mainly greens and pinks. (Street lights are confined to the foreshore, so our night skies are unaffected.)

Helen
STEWART ISLAND

ALTHOUGH the sun always rises in an easterly quarter, in winter the point of rising is nearly south east.

Special cloud formations appear in winter. In the southern districts, heavy, steely blue clouds form on the horizon as a forewarning of snow.

Different star constellations can best be seen at various times of the year. To the Maori, who particularly watched the dawn sky, the appearance of Pleiades, known by them as Matariki (Little Eyes), heralded the beginning of the new year, in the middle of June. Rigel (Puanga), the brightest star of Orion, and the belt of Orion (Tautoro), are seen rising in the early morning sky of June and July.

Near Orion, the bright star Sirius, called Takurua by the Maori, is also seen in the early hours of cold winter mornings. A Maori proverb, 'te anu o Takurua' (the cold of Takurua) reflects their belief that Takurua heralded cold and snow. Takurua is also their word for winter. It was thought that if Takurua was shining brightly, it was a sign of a severe frost.

The zodiacal constellations that can be seen in the early evening are: Sagittarius, Scorpius, Libra, Virgo and Leo. Later in the night, Pisces, Aquarius and Capricornus can be seen.

Sirius is the brightest star in this cluster showing Hyades and Orion

Aurora Australis over Auckland

Sperm whale

THE SEAS AND RIVERS

THE winter storms whip up the ocean and pound onto the beaches, bringing driftwood and seaweed. The colder currents from Antarctica push their way north, up the east and west coasts. This affects all the fish and other marine creatures in different ways.

There is no plankton growth in winter, because the light from the sun is much weaker, and the water is colder. Many of the various fish species around New Zealand are known to spawn in the ocean during the winter months, after the 'second spring' blooming of plankton in the autumn.

Some examples of winter-spawning fish are hoki and groper (the two species: hapuka and bass), which seem to spawn earlier in the north than in the south. Orange roughy spawn in very deep water in special spawning grounds.

Most of the commercial harvesting of the deep-sea fish species happens in winter. Species include hoki, hake, ling, southern blue whiting, cardinal fish, warehou, orange roughy, and the oreo dories.

The snapper disappear from their summer feeding grounds, and kahawai are found in deeper water offshore during winter. In winter, blue-nosed dolphins are sighted coming into many northern harbours. They come to feed on kahawai which are in turn feeding on whitebait.

Crayfish are carrying eggs. Winter is also when the crayfish boats go to sea. In July, crayfishermen are busy preparing their pots, which are rectangular metal frames and need to be painted with zinc to prevent corrosion. Ropes are measured, floats checked, and the boats sail away for their owners' particular fishing places.

Humpback whales migrate up the east coast on their way to Tonga. The sperm whales which live in the waters around Kaikoura move away from the shore during winter.

In the inland rivers, trout return downstream after spawning in the shallow rivers upstream.

I love the foam that normally comes onto the beach in winter. It is like a giant natural bubble bath.

Malcolm
WESTPORT

———

Trout spawn in winter, and when they travel back downstream from the headwaters where they have mated we can't fish for them.

Joseph
HAWKE'S BAY

Piles of shingle
are brought to the
beaches during
winter storms.

Rick
HIKURANGI,
NORTHLAND

———————

July brings the
easterly, blowing
straight into
Halfmoon Bay, where
most of the fishing
fleet float at their
moorings. This is
the wind the fishermen
dread, as a broken
mooring chain will
mean the boat ends up
on the beach — in
pieces.

Helen
STEWART ISLAND

Crayfish

THE LAND

There are lots of
puddles and mud.
We get ice off the
puddles, but we don't
play outside much.

George and Erin
EKETAHUNA,
MANAWATU

————————

The white sparkly
snow covers the
ground like white
concrete, and the
grader pushes the
snow up to the side
of the road into
a big bank. Inside
we have the fires
crackling to warm
my toes.

Tamara
LAKE TEKAPO,
SOUTH CANTERBURY

SNOW falls on many mountains and ranges. In the South Island the rivers become low, or dry up, due to the heavy snow and hard frost in the Southern Alps. The mountains all over New Zealand have snow on them at some stage during winter. On some of the bigger mountains there is a lot of snow, and some of these are popular places for skiing.

Sometimes major highways can be closed because of snow, particularly in the South Island, but also roads such as the Desert Road in the Central Plateau of the North Island.

The inland lakes become very cold, and some ponds and small lakes in the South Island ice over.

However, there are often clear days when the sun shines, although not as strongly as it does in summer. On these sunny days, there are usually frosts to wake up to in the mornings. Children like to go out and break the ice off the puddles and crunch through the stiff grass, and enjoy watching their breath appear as great clouds of steam.

Mist and fog patches hang around longer in winter, especially in the bush. Night-time air cooling takes longer in winter so the mist has more time to form.

Deciduous trees lose their leaves. Their bare branches, with their differing forms, look beautiful against the wintry sky. The young branches of some types of willow are a striking red, orange or golden colour.

Kiwifruit and parsnips ripen. Winter is the best time for tree planting because they can grow stronger roots.

Malcolm
WESTPORT

———————

In winter, Daddy ploughs the paddocks for crops like wheat. I run along between the furrows.

Tim
TIMARU

Although most introduced plants flower in the spring, there are a number of winter-flowering plants and trees. The scent and colour of pink daphne and violets delight the senses, while brightly coloured polyanthus is another cheerful sight in winter gardens. Rhododendrons and camellias are very colourful shrubs which flower in the later part of winter.

Almond trees blossom and tall wattle trees have a blaze of yellow flowers, while other trees around them are stark and wintry still.

Not long after mid-winter, early bulbs begin to appear, and these continue through into spring. Tiny blossom buds start forming on the fruit trees. Pine trees flower in July, shedding clouds of pollen over everything.

Late in winter the kaka beak flowers. (Although this is actually a native plant it is only found in cultivated gardens now.) The gorse also starts flowering at this time, providing a good feed for hungry bees.

Kaka beak flowers

THE NATIVE FORESTS

UNLIKE the Northern Hemisphere, most of New Zealand's native trees are evergreens, which means they do not lose their leaves in winter. There are, however, a few which do, such as the native fuchsia (kotukutuku), the lacebark (houhere), and the mountain ribbonwood (manatu).

The kowhai tree also loses its leaves just before it flowers again in spring. If you study the small branches of the trees, you will notice that tiny leaf buds have already formed.

One of the most wonderful winter happenings is the flowering of the kohekohe tree. This handsome tree has beautiful sprays of white, sweet-smelling flowers, which spring from the trunk of the tree as well as the branches. Flowering begins in mid-winter, although often earlier in the north. In July the karaka trees flower.

The puriri tree flowers all year round but especially so from June through to the middle of spring. Many of the small native orchids flower in winter. The green hooded orchids come out first and later the spider orchids.

Winter is when the mosses and lichens, liverworts and filmy ferns look their best. These plants can shrivel up when it is dry in the bush, as it often can be in summer and autumn. But with the moist, damp conditions of winter, they come to life and look very beautiful.

Winter is also the best time of the year to look for different fungi in the bush. New Zealand has a range of colourful fungi.

Spleenwort (top)

Green-hooded orchid (left)

Entoloma hochstetteri *toadstools* (opposite top)

In winter, the Ruahine bush is wet and dark and cold. Often there is a biting wind from the peaks, and we love to tramp up to the snow.

Chris
CENTRAL HAWKE'S BAY

The bush is really wet when we go tramping in winter. We get soaked even when it's not raining, because we have to brush past bushes that are soaked.

Joe
WAITAKERE,
AUCKLAND

THE BIRDS

THE early part of winter is a relatively quiet time for birdlife. The birds that have migrated north or overseas have left by the end of autumn. Some types of birds, like the finches, starlings and silvereyes, form flocks. Many birds move about the country, away from colder regions.

Silvereyes (also known as waxeyes) leave the higher altitudes and turn up in the milder lowland and coastal areas, looking for berries, such as fuchsia and five finger. They also enjoy treats, such as breadcrumbs and fat, put out by bird-lovers in their home gardens.

Silvereyes

The bellbirds come to where we live at Leithfield beach in the autumn. They come from Mt Grey and stay over winter, because it is too cold for them up there. They make a bell-like sound and are pleasant to have around. If you put honey and water out for them in the trees, they come to drink it. They sit in the banksia trees and sing a happy song.

Luke
LEITHFIELD BEACH,
NORTH CANTERBURY

Bellbird (right)

Yellowhammers

Bellbirds leave their summer mountain homes and come down to the warmer regions to feed. Their bell-like calls are welcomed by people who leave honey water out for them to drink.

Flocks of cheeky chaffinches turn up in many places, searching for fallen seed from crops and roadside grasses. Yellowhammers eat the seeds that fall from the hay fed out to cattle on farms. They also visit many populated town areas.

In winter, hawks can be seen circling, looking for prey. Fantails flit about in the open spaces between bare winter branches.

Later in the season many species of birds begin mating and nesting activities. The little blue penguins start coming ashore and making their burrows. Paradise ducks begin building their nests, calling out to each other.

The takahe also begin nest building. Male gannets return to the gannetries, which are last year's nesting sites, and wait for their mates to arrive.

Harrier hawk

```
We get ready for
winter early.
When we see the
snowbirds on the
grapevines we know
that snow is
coming soon.

William
WAIKAIA,
SOUTHLAND
```

```
In winter the little
blue penguins are
more noticeable as
they come ashore to
breed. We sit and
watch for them as
they walk like little
old men up to their
burrows. We pity the
poor crib owners with
penguins underneath
because they bray
like donkeys.

Helen
STEWART ISLAND
```

Blue penguin in its nest with chicks

THE ANIMALS

WINTER is a resting time for most creatures. Most birds and animals seem to be hiding.

Lizards and tuataras are hibernating. They are cold-blooded and need external warmth, so when it is cold they slow down or sleep. Frogs hibernate, too, for the same reason.

Tuatara

Monarch butterflies

Insects are in a largely dormant state as well. Some simply hide out during winter, and others slow down their development while they wait for warmer weather. Red admiral butterflies find a crevice in the bark of a tree and stay there during the colder weather. Sometimes, in the middle of a warm sunny day in winter, they come out for a brief airing. Other butterflies, such as the monarchs, will hide on the underside of branches, and likewise come out briefly on sunny days.

Domestic and farm animals grow warm winter coats, and seek out warm places in which to 'hide'. Cattle and dairy cows start calving, and 'early' lambs are born in the late winter.

In the bush, wild deer and possums also grow thick coats. Mice and rats try to come into houses looking for warm places to nest.

The grazing pattern of cattle changes during unsettled weather. Normally they have very established patterns and lie down at the same time every day to sleep. However, just before there is a storm they will not have their normal rest but continue grazing. Hedgehogs can also be seen out in the open during the day, building up reserves for the stormy time ahead.

Every winter the pond
below our house
freezes up and talks
in a creaking sound.
When it is thick
we skate on it.
The ducks walk around
on ice looking for a
place to swim and
feed. Each morning
Dad goes to feed the
hungry stock. He
feeds them all the
round hay bales and
oats we made in
summer.

Alana
LAKE TEKAPO,
SOUTH CANTERBURY

THE PEOPLE

BECAUSE of the cold weather, winter is an indoors time. People themselves become more inward. They spend more time reading and finding activities to do inside. People with fires like to sit in front of them, and warm themselves 'through to the bone'.

Farmers have to feed out hay to their animals. Winter is the 'no-growth' time of the year for grass, so the animals get hungry and have to be fed with hay. Other farm work in winter includes fencing and general maintenance, such as fixing gates. In some places ploughing for spring-crop planting is done in winter. Kiwifruit is harvested before the possums and silvereyes can eat them.

Winter is cold, wet and damp. I like to sit by a fire and warm my feet and hands. When I go out to play I put on my fleecy jacket, hat, woollen mittens and long rubber boots.

Rebecca
KAITAIA,
NORTHLAND

_____

Winter means playing more inside games; board and card games. It also means reading more books. I get bored playing inside. I get grouchy because I can't go surfing, but I get excited about going skiing.

William
WAIKAIA,
SOUTHLAND

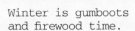

Gardeners plant out young trees and roses, when the sap is in the roots. They get their soil ready, too, for the spring growth time ahead. In the vegetable garden, broad beans are sown, and garlic is planted at mid-winter.

In marinas and boat-yards, many boats are brought up into the dry docks. People work on them, scraping, repairing and repainting them in readiness for the summer sailing ahead.

People play vigorous sports in winter, like rugby, soccer, netball and hockey, or they go ice-skating, tobogganing and skiing. Children who live near snow have a lot of fun playing in it.

Winter is gumboots
and firewood time.

Tui
NORTHLAND

————————

We start feeding out
when the snow falls.
I go snow yakking
with Dad. The snow is
so deep, sometimes up
to my waist. I lie on
it and roll down the
hill.
We lose our water.
The roads get icy. We
often get bad colds.

Brylee
GLENORCHY,
SOUTHLAND

SPRING
Koanga, Mahuru

IN the Southern Hemisphere, spring officially begins on the first day of September. The spring equinox is between 20 and 23 September.

However, spring-like activities happen well before this. Many bird species begin nesting in August, and some even earlier. Spring bulbs burst into bloom throughout August. In many places lambs are being born and grass has begun growing again while it is still 'officially' winter.

Spring is one of the two 'in-between' seasons. It could be described as an 'adolescent' season. The length of the days and nights are relatively equal. Spring is also a changeover time from the coldest part of the year, when the country is furthest away from the sun, and the hottest time of the year, when it is nearest the sun.

It is not surprising, then, that spring weather is a mixture of hot and cold. The weather is very changeable. Sometimes it is warm and sunny, then quite quickly it can become cold and showery, sending animals and people running for shelter.

Occasionally, in the colder parts of the country, there are even snowstorms which would normally be thought of as belonging only to winter. Frosts can occur up until October and 'unseasonable' late frosts can threaten orchard crops or frost-tender young plants even in November.

Every year, strong winds called equinoctials arrive during spring. In most parts of the country the winds are from a westerly direction. These are created by the transition of high pressure from the north meeting low pressure from the south. The winds occur as the tail end of a weather pattern driving northward from the south, and they gradually weaken and die out the further north they go.

The air smells sweeter in spring than at any other time of the year. This is because there are so many flowers and young leaves unfolding and growing.

Life flows into everything.

William
DANNEVIRKE,
HAWKE'S BAY

The streams and rivers are freezing in spring, because of all the snow melting. I love to have a quick swim in them, because when I come out, my skin is tingling.

Chris
CENTRAL HAWKE'S BAY

The wind swishes through the trees and makes a whining sound at the windows. Sometimes a Nor'wester blows the chimney pot off and you can hear a clattering sound as it blows down the roof.

Alana
LAKE TEKAPO,
SOUTH CANTERBURY

Location	Rainfall Total (mm) mean monthly	Temperature Mean daily maximum °C	Sunshine Mean hours per day	Relative Humidity Mean daily (%)
Auckland	96	18.3	5.8	77
Napier	55	19.0	6.6	67
Ruapehu	264	10.9	5.2	84
Wellington	99	15.2	6.2	80
Nelson	84	16.7	6.8	76
Christchurch	47	17.3	6.3	74
Dunedin	59	14.8	4.9	72

THE SKY

MACKEREL clouds are often seen in spring. A Maori proverb, 'Mara kumara a Nga-toro-i-rangi', likened this type of cloud formation to the kumara mounds of the great priest, Nga-toro-i-rangi. The mackerel clouds are seen in summer and autumn as well, and indicate fair weather ahead.

Mares' tails (cirrus clouds) are also often seen in spring. They are signs of strong winds, and when they are seen in the sky it means there will be beautiful sunsets or sunrises.

Spring is an especially good time to see arching rainbows. The scattered showers and cumulus clouds of late spring and summer produce the best conditions for them. The highest arches occur when the sun is lower in the sky.

We watch for mares'
tails in the sky at
the end of spring,
because then we
know it is time to
plant our kumara.

Chris
CENTRAL HAWKE'S BAY

Small Magellanic cloud

In spring the Magellanic clouds can be seen high in the sky, especially on dark nights. These are actually other galaxies which look like wispy clouds of light. They were known to the Maori as Tioreore and Tikatakata, and were said to protect people from heavy winds.

Canopus, known as Aotahi to the Maori, can be seen in the early morning in spring. Rigel (Puanga) is also seen in the morning, now in the northern part of the sky.

In the early evening in spring, the zodiacal constellations to be seen are: Pisces, Aquarius, Capricornus, Sagittarius, Scorpius and Libra. In the early morning, Gemini, Taurus and Aries are visible.

The skies are very moody in spring. One minute there is not a cloud to be seen in the sky, and the next, there is not a patch of blue to be seen!

Beth
DEVONPORT,
AUCKLAND

THE SEAS AND RIVERS

A favourite spring arrival are the dolphins, bringing their new babies. They come to the sheltered bays to give their new 'pupils' fishing lessons. Fishermen are to be seen setting for flounder more frequently and magnificent gannets can be seen dive-bombing the increasing numbers of fish.

Ruth
NORTHLAND

———

Spring is also the start of the salmon kill, which is a change for the crews from the endless round of chores such as filling the feeders and chasing the seals away.

Helen
STEWART ISLAND

———

Whitebait swim up the rivers... this means we can have whitebait fritters. Seals come closer to the shore to feed.

Misha
WESTPORT

FROM a land perspective the sea seems to 'lag behind' in spring. The rhythms of the sea are quite different from those on shore. Later in the season, as the water begins to warm up, the light gets brighter and there are more sunlight hours. The phytoplankton begin to bloom.

Once the plankton have bloomed, a whole chain of development can and does occur, because the food chain in the ocean is very interdependent. The simple plankton is the first stage of this development. Marine life then increases noticeably.

Different activities are happening in different parts of New Zealand. After the moki have finished spawning in the East Cape region, they travel south again to spend the warmer months near Kaikoura in the South Island.

Snapper are serial spawners, and begin releasing their batches of eggs in spring. School shark pups are 'released' into nurseries in sheltered coasts and shallow bays in spring and early summer.

Bottlenose dolphins

The male crayfish (rock lobster) sheds his shell (moults), so that a larger one can grow. This usually takes place in late spring and early summer. The female moult takes place in autumn.

Whale strandings often occur in the North Island during the late August and September equinoctial storms of spring. The pilot whales migrate up the east coast of the North Island at this time. Sightings of whales from the shore are quite common during these months.

In spring the trout start rising in the rivers and the lakes. They have come down from their spawning grounds, and are actively seeking food.

The whitebait are running upstream in the rivers from the ocean, heading back to their spawning grounds.

The spring melt is on and the rivers are high.
The whitebait are running up the rivers. In the sea the kahawai are chasing the whitebait.
The oystercatchers, the paradise ducks and the banded dotterels are nesting on the beach. The Fiordland crested penguins nest above the beach.

Jennifer, Sam and Elinor
BARN BAY,
SOUTH WESTLAND

Whitebait

THE LAND

AS heat comes back into the sun, and the earth starts to warm up, seeds sprout and plants and trees start growing again. Spring is the growth time of the year.

The days start getting noticeably longer, with dawn arriving earlier and dusk later.

The snow on the mountain ranges starts melting, which makes the river levels rise, often very high. The equinoctial winds assist the melt, and can also dry out the ground. In some places this is welcome, but these winds can burn young leaves and blow off the blossoms or the newly setting fruit. They can also create big waves on seas and on inland lakes.

Spring is very evident in plants and trees which derive from the Northern Hemisphere. All the deciduous trees which had lost their leaves before winter are now covered in tiny bursting buds, which very quickly become soft pretty leaves.

Many fruit trees burst into blossom before they grow leaves. Fruit orchards are a very colourful sight with rows and rows of trees in blossom.

In spring the
new shoots come
out of the trees.

Rose
RAUMATI,
KAPITI COAST

I love spring
because all the
blossom trees
come out and we
sometimes pick
branches to put
in the house.

Hannah
HAWKE'S BAY

It seems as if every day more varieties of flowers appear, filling the air with sweetness. Freesias, jasmine and wisteria are just some of the lovely scented plants which are seen in gardens. Bright tulips and anemones appear, and later in spring the rose season begins.

On banks and 'wasteland', wild flowers appear.

The snowdrops in August herald the beginning of spring, and they are usually all gone before the daffodils come out. When the Nor-West winds start, the snow begins to melt on the tops, and the rivers start to flood. During some springs we have only been able to cross our river on about one day in ten. We try to get our crutching done between showers, before lambing starts in October.

Sally
MT ALGIDUS,
CANTERBURY

The fuchsia trees,
the wine berry, the
bush lawyer, and
the native clematis
are all in flower.
The coprosma
berries are
starting to set.

Jennifer, Sam and
Elinor
BARN BAY,
SOUTH WESTLAND

MANY native plants and trees flower at this time of year. One symbol that heralds the arrival of spring is the native clematis (puawhananga). Its delicate swathes of snowy white flowers appear high in the tree-tops late in winter, and continue flowering into spring.

Probably the most beloved of all sights among native plants in spring is the kowhai, with its masses of large, yellow, bell-like flowers. The kowhai trees start flowering in September, and are fully out by Labour Day (late October).

The sweet-smelling kohuhu flowers, which are dark purple, and the small, sweetly scented mahoe both appear in September. The long flowering seasons of the manuka, followed by the kanuka, start in September.

The native fuchsia (kotukutuku) flowers in October and bees are busy gathering its fascinating blue pollen. The cabbage tree also begins to blossom in October, with large branches of strongly scented white flowers.

Native clematis flowers

Manuka flowers (right)

Rewarewa trees start producing their spectacular red-brown flowers with yellow centres in spring, too.

As well as many flowers which appear in the native bush in spring, there are striking happenings in the fern world.

On the forest floor new, bright green crown fern (piu piu) fronds start uncurling from spring onwards. The ponga and mamaku ferns also uncurl their fronds.

Pretty bronze bracken (rauaruhe) begins popping up and uncurling, but this is not a welcome sight to farmers. They wage war on the bracken so there is more grass for their sheep, or, in the case of goats, so that their animals don't get poisoned by eating the plant.

As new leaves break through on the beech trees, the old leaves fall. They turn a beautiful red, yellow and brown, creating a bright carpet on the beech forest floor.

Rewarewa flowers (top)

Ponga fern (above)

I always love the bush in spring because it smells so clean and earthy, and somehow I take more notice of rain droplets hanging from ferns and trees. When the sun shines they glisten like little crystals.

Beth
HAWKE'S BAY

Beech forest

THE BIRDS

SPRING is a time of great activity for birds. Almost all of them are taking part in the breeding process during this season, although some species have already started in winter. The various activities of the breeding season are fun to watch: the mating rituals, nest building, the laying and incubating of eggs, and the feeding and guarding of chicks.

Another exciting bird event in spring is the arrival of migratory birds from the Northern Hemisphere. They come to feed during the New Zealand spring and summer, and prepare for their flight home in time for their breeding season in the northern spring.

Godwits (kuaka) are one of the main migratory birds. They arrive from Siberia in huge flocks, looking very lean and drab. The birds spread themselves throughout New Zealand, feeding mainly in the coastal wetlands, mudflats and estuaries, although the greatest concentrations are in the northern harbours and at Farewell Spit in Golden Bay.

The tuis party on the sweet nectar of the kowhai, which start to flower at the beginning of spring and are in full flower by October. Pairs of oystercatchers start coming back in early spring.

Ruth
NORTHLAND

Takahe mating displays occur from August through to October. Takahe chicks are sighted from the beginning of September on. Both male and female birds feed the chicks.

Jann
MANA ISLAND,
WELLINGTON

Hen blackbird feeding chicks

Tui feeding on kowhai (above left)

Shining cuckoo

The call of the
shining cuckoo is
first heard in
September, but the
bird is seldom
seen. We know it
signals the hope of
summer to come.
In November the
fluffy blue-black
ducklings can be
seen with their
parents swimming
upstream in the
free-flowing, clear
mountain rivers and
streams.

Jane
KING COUNTRY,
WAIKATO

Another migratory bird is the shining cuckoo (pipi-wharaaroa), which flies down from the Solomon Islands or the nearby Bismarck Archipelago. The call of the pipiwhararoa is a most welcome sound, as its return to New Zealand is seen as a definite sign that spring has arrived. A Maori proverb confirms this: 'Ka tangi te pipiwhararoa, ko nga karere a Mahuru' (When the shining cuckoo sings, he is the messenger of spring). Unfortunately this beautiful bird is rarely seen.

Unlike the other bird visitors, the pipiwhararoa comes here to breed. Because it is a cuckoo, the bird lays its egg in the nest of an unsuspecting 'host'. Its favourite host is the grey warbler (riroriro) which completes its first nesting before the pipiwhararoa have arrived. This is just as well for the host bird's survival as a species, because when the baby cuckoo is hatched, it gets rid of its rivals and goes on to exhaust its foster parents with its demands.

There are many internal migratory patterns, as various bird species return to their favourite areas to breed and feed on their preferred delicacies. People living in Northland and Canterbury have recorded the return of oystercatchers in early spring.

In gannetries, the gannets are gathered, and their mating and nesting rituals are among the most spectacular to observe.

Gannets

THE ANIMALS

In spring the rivers begin to flow, and the chamois coats turn white. The oystercatchers and dotterels return.

Lil
EREWHON STATION,
CANTERBURY

SPRING is the growth time of the year for everything, including animals. Many farm animals are giving birth and feeding their babies. New lambs and calves appear in the paddocks every day. They are all eating the spring grass and growing.

Deer, both in the bush and on farms, are giving birth to fawns. Pets such as cats and dogs are also having their litters of kittens and puppies.

Hibernating animals, such as the tuatara and lizards, start to wake up.

Baby tadpoles appear in dams and water troughs. As they mature, they grow little legs and transform into frogs. Frogs can be heard croaking throughout the day. At night their croaking turns into a type of 'singing', or 'roaring' if there are large numbers of them.

Common blue butterfly

Insects start appearing everywhere. Bees don't start getting active until the average daily temperature is at least 10°C. Once it is warm enough, they become very busy gathering nectar and pollen. They can often be seen swarming at this time of the year.

Beautiful butterflies start appearing in gardens and in the bush as spring advances. Spiders are seen more often as well, with some venturing into houses, and, in the case of the black tunnelweb and nursery web spider, causing some alarm!

```
Spring sun shining
brightly onto the
earth. Ponds filled
with baby ducklings.
Rabbits leaping
over fallen trees.
Islands filled with
birds chirping.
Newborn babies here
at last. The growth
time of the year.

Rebecca
KAITAIA,
NORTHLAND
```

Nursery web spider

THE PEOPLE

SPRING is an active season. All the growth in nature and the warming of the temperature combine to make people more active. People often experience an uplift in spirits.

Spring is very busy for anyone whose work is related to the soil. Gardeners start planting seeds and planting out seedlings. In gardens all over the country, flowers are unfolding, and vegetables are growing again.

Farmers are sowing their summer crops.

On farms, young animals, such as calves, lambs, fawns and kids, are being born. Spring is the time of year for pet lambs, as there are always motherless lambs that need looking after.

In spring, plants are growing. It's getting warmer and I like going outside again.

Erin
EKETAHUNA,
MANAWATU

We burn the fern so the sheep have more grass.
There are often floods. Once our road was washed out and we couldn't get out for weeks.
We can't use our boat so much because the wind is really bad. The lake gets very rough. One year the waves were as high as the house, and windows were broken.

Brylee
GLENORCHY,
SOUTHLAND

Later on in the season, farmers start docking the lambs' tails. Then the sheep are crutched and dagged, in preparation for shearing off the heavy winter coats in early summer.

Children enjoy playing outside once more. They are like the lambs at evening-time, skipping and prancing around in the fresh-smelling air.

The days get longer, so we can stay outside longer. Everyone seems happier, because it's warmer, bouncier, prettier.

Misha
WESTPORT

In spring I always get a pet lamb that is left over at the end of lambing. We start up the lamb warming box and feed sick lambs.

Tim
TIMARU

In spring, people 'come out of hibernation', and neighbours start chatting to each other again as they get outside and work in their gardens.

Beth
DEVONPORT,
AUCKLAND

SUMMER
Raumati

Pohutukav...

The nights are
shorter and the days
are longer.
I can play much
longer after tea.
There is a lot of
fruit. I eat plums
and more plums.

Christopher
AUCKLAND

I love summer because
there are birds
singing all day in
our big macrocarpa
trees. When I wake up
in the morning,
sometimes the sound
is deafening. We
always go down to the
river and swim for
hours. We bomb off
the willow branches
into the river, and
then we get out and
lie on the warm
stones, and listen to
the river rippling
over the rapids.

Rachel
CENTRAL HAWKE'S BAY

SUMMER officially begins on the first day of December. The summer solstice is just before Christmas, between 20 and 23 December. This is the longest day of the year with the largest amount of daylight hours. In summer the length of the day is longer than the length of the night.

After this solstice, even though summer scarcely seems to have begun, we are slowly heading back towards winter. Although it won't be noticed for some time, the days are gradually getting shorter.

Summer is the hottest time of the year, although temperatures are generally mild. However, because New Zealand consists of two main islands, the climate is not always settled. Summer storms and rainy weather often occur in many parts of the country.

In the North there are often strong easterly winds in December, which bring a large amount of rain.
Coastal regions in New Zealand can often be humid in summer. This means the air is heavy with moisture.

Temperatures often reach the 30s in many parts of the country. As the summer progresses, some drought-prone areas, such as Hawke's Bay and Otago, can experience very high temperatures.

Due to 'seasonal lag', the best summer weather happens well after the solstice. The hottest and most settled weather is usually in late January and February.

Lupin flowers cover the roadsides for miles around. The tourists stop to take photos of them. Summer is very busy for us on the farm. We have to make big round bales of hay for the sheep to eat in winter.
We also have to harvest the oat crops.
We spend hours each day picking raspberries to eat with cream, and for Mum to preserve. Sometimes we pick the red and blackcurrants to put in the freezer for drinks in winter. Best of all, we have long holidays and I don't have to spend my mornings doing a story.

Alana
LAKE TEKAPO,
SOUTH CANTERBURY

Location	Rainfall Total (mm) mean monthly	Temperature Mean daily maximum °C	Sunshine Mean hours per day	Relative Humidity Mean daily (%)
Auckland	83	23.3	7.3	76
Napier	57	23.7	7.4	68
Ruapehu	199	17.0	6.9	80
Wellington	76	19.9	7.5	79
Nelson	72	21.7	8.1	74
Christchurch	44	22.0	7.0	74
Dunedin	67	18.5	5.5	74

THE SKY

IN summer the rising sun is in the north east. The rays of the sun are at their most intense in summer.
Sometimes great cumulonimbus clouds (thunderheads) are seen in the sky, forecasting summer thunderstorms. Fluffy cotton-wool or cumulus clouds, however, are a sign of good weather.

The sun is very hot and it dries up the hills and the rivers. Trout fishermen love summer because of the long dusks full of all the insects that have hatched.

Chris
CENTRAL HAWKE'S BAY

At the beginning of summer Scorpius is seen above the horizon in the early morning sky. The Maori used to read it as a sign that summer was coming. Antares, which is the bright star in Scorpius, was known as Rehua and a Maori proverb, 'Kua tahu a Rehua' (Rehua has burnt, or kindled), referred to the star as the sign of summer.
Another sign seen in the early morning sky in early summer is Castor and Pollux. These bright twin stars of Gemini can be seen in the northern part of the sky.

The constellation of Orion is very bright in the summer night skies. This cluster of stars has become known as 'the Pot'. Sirius and Aldebaran, on either side of Orion, are also prominent. The Pleiades cluster is seen over to the west.

The zodiacal constellations that can be seen in the earlier part of the evening are: Gemini, Taurus, Aries, Pisces and Aquarius. Later in the evening, Virgo, Leo and Cancer can be seen.

Constellation of Scorpius, showing Jupiter as brightest star and Antares as second brightest

THE algal blooms, which have been occurring from late spring onwards in recent years, may colour the sea by summer. The water can appear yellow-green, brownish or even at times reddish, according to which algae are predominant.

The school snapper start coming into New Zealand's more shallow, sheltered coastal waters. Large schools of mature snapper congregate before spawning and move together to the spawning grounds from spring through to summer.

Bigger shoals of small fish come in close to shore in summer. Sometimes big fish like the kingfish chase after them. When the kingfish start arriving, gannets and seagulls can be seen hovering in huge flocks, especially when the fish start 'chopping'. (This is a fish frenzy, with little fish being chased by larger fish.)

The main season for many of the inshore species of fish is during the late spring and summer months when they are pursued by both commercial and recreational fishermen.

Jellyfish appear in beaches and bays. Some of them can inflict very painful and poisonous stings. Squid eggs sometimes get washed up during summer. They appear in large clumps of sausage-like capsules.

The common blue-bottle jellyfish come in great numbers. When we drive our boat through the water, you can hear the prop on the outboard slowing up as it fights to turn, because the jellyfish are so thick. The beaches have so many jellyfish sometimes, you can't swim there. Then the children enjoy a good old-fashioned jellyfish fight. However the man-of-war is not so pleasant and can cause some very allergic reactions. These are also plentiful in summer and we have to watch carefully for them.

Shay and Bevan
PICTON

In summer we get whale strandings every year. Golden Bay is called one of the world's worst whale traps.

Rowan
GOLDEN BAY,
NELSON

———

Near the salmon farms we can see seals spinning in the water. They lie on the surface and spin over and over while moving forward slowly. This seems to be a pleasure activity.

Helen
STEWART ISLAND

Many whale strandings occur around Farewell Spit during the summer months, often over the Christmas and New Year period. The pilot whales are migrating through Cook Strait at this time.

In the inland waterways, eels are sometimes seen gliding slowly in the streams. Baby eels can be seen at night in their thousands foraging on the river bottom.

Trout tend to lie low in the deeper and colder waters of the river. Being cold-blooded they don't like the warmer waters, although they will come into the shallows in the evening to feed.

THE LAND

It's nice and hot
and we can swim all
the time. There are
lots of fresh fruit
and vegetables.

William
DANNEVIRKE,
HAWKE'S BAY

_____

In summer we
harvest the crops.
Daddy heads wheat,
barley, oats, peas,
clover and ryegrass
with the header.
He has to test the
crops to see if
they are ready.
He uses a moisture
meter and it grinds
the wheat and makes
little cakes. I like
eating them.
We have to grub the
nodding thistles.
I like spotting
nodders, and run
along by the truck
looking for them.
Mummy or Daddy grub
them out. Nodding
thistles are light
green and silvery.
They have little
prickly bits.

Tim
TIMARU

_____

Summer is dusty.
We go to the creek
to swim and catch
eels. The hills are
brown and hard.

George and Erin
EKETAHUNA,
MANAWATU

AT this time of year the mountains have very little snow on them and the alpine flowers are in full bloom. Everything on the land is at its peak: trees are in full leaf and flowers are everywhere.

The sun sets as much as an hour later in the south than in the north and the dusk lingers for longer. A number of flowering trees and plants give off their scent as night falls, making the long warm evenings even more pleasant.

All the deciduous trees are in full leaf throughout summer. Wildflowers are seen on roadsides all over the country.

In the North Island, purple convolvulus and water lilies start blooming in early summer. The hills around Wellington are covered in a variety of wildflowers, many of them 'escapees' from cultivated gardens. In the South Island, the colourful lupins bloom.

Drought areas start to look increasingly brown as the season progresses. There is more risk of accidental fires on the land, in the forests or grasslands, as everything dries out.

In summer you can hear the gorse seeds popping.

Joseph
HAWKE'S BAY

In summer our blocks are covered in white clover flowers for the sheep to eat. Weaning is a busy time for all of us. All the lambs have to be taken away from their mums and they cry sadly.

Tamara
LAKE TEKAPO,
SOUTH CANTERBURY

THE NATIVE FORESTS

IN summer many species of native trees and shrubs are either flowering or developing their fruit (berries). The flax bushes flower and attract tuis to feed on their nectar. The feathery flowers of the toi tois are out.

The pohutukawa tree, which grows best near the coasts of the North Island, produces the most spectacular display of red flowers. The northern and the southern rata also have a very showy display of similar red flowers.

The lovely kamahi flowers in the earlier part of summer, and the many different varieties of hebes – native shrubs – flower throughout summer.

The manuka and kanuka, which began flowering in spring, are in full flower throughout summer and the pretty nikau palm also flowers all season.

The glorious pohutukawa trees (New Zealand's Christmas tree) bloom in summer. An old Maori proverb refers to the early blooming of the pohutukawa, as indicating a long dry summer.

Rick
HIKURANGI,
NORTHLAND

Walking through the bush in summer makes me feel refreshed, because it is cool and shady. In late summer the earth is quite dry underneath.

Beth
HAWKE'S BAY

In mountain regions, beautiful summer alpine flowers are out. Even though it is summer, they have to be very hardy to endure changing conditions. Mountain orchids are blooming, too.

In summer the rata, the kamahi and the flax are in flower. The fuchsia berries are formed, and the tutu berries are ripe.

Jennifer, Sam and Elinor
BARN BAY,
SOUTH WESTLAND

In summer we see the snow tussock flowers and the mountain daisy (celmisia) flowers. In late summer, the oystercatchers and dotterels leave.

Lil
EREWHON STATION,
CANTERBURY

Berries, such as the karaka, tawa, totara, miro and matai, and the wineberry (makomako), are forming on many trees all through summer. Some berries are ready for eating by mid-summer and native pigeons and other birds travel from one source of berries to another.

THE BIRDS

We have the rare native spotted dotterel breeding in early summer near us. They lay their eggs in the middle of the sand, and storms have sometimes come and washed their nests away.

Rick
HIKURANGI,
NORTHLAND

IN summer, the young birds that hatched in spring start to appear — to feed and develop. Many species of birds have more than one brood so they are busy feeding their new chicks. Some species of birds, such as the dotterels, don't begin nesting until summer.

The nests are very noisy with the happy chirping and to-ing and fro-ing of parent birds. The chirping in large trees which have many nests can be quite deafening!

As the chicks develop they start learning how to fly, or, in the case of penguins, learning to swim.

Gannet colonies are an amazing sight in summer with huge numbers of parent birds and fledglings. The baby gannets start their wing practice a long time before they try to take off.

The shining cuckoo chicks grow fatter and more demanding of their unwitting foster parents, until it is their time to fly out on their own. Before summer is over the birds begin to leave New Zealand to fly back to their northern homes.

New Zealand dotterel

Summer sees the young birds appear, feed and develop. Late summer sees the fantails display their skillful hovering dances on the verandah enjoying the nectar from the honeysuckle.

Rowena and Grant
BLENHEIM

Fantail

All over the country, the migratory visitors from the Northern Hemisphere, such as the oystercatchers, bar-tailed godwits and knots, can be seen feeding on the mudflats. They are fattening up for their journey back home in New Zealand's autumn.

Summer is when the remarkable mating displays of the kakapo take place. The male kakapo starts his 'booming' in December and January. The 'track and bowl' building takes shape in January. By February the booming has intensified, which eventually (all going well) attracts a female.

In late summer new ducklings have almost all their adult plumage; only a small patch of down remains between the wings.

After they have finished nesting, many different varieties of ducks and geese gather in very secluded places for the summer moult. There are often huge congregations of one species in the same place.

Oystercatchers

In early summer the oystercatchers start to lay eggs. When the chicks hatch you have to duck down or they will dive-bomb you.

Amiria
WESTPORT

———

Summer is boating and fishing time, and diving for scallops, and paua. The terns are seen hovering over the pleasure fishing boats in the harbour. We see the odd gannet. Tuis get into the flax flowers by Christmas time. The starlings also enjoy them. Mutton-birds lay their eggs in late spring, early summer. The little blue penguins brood their young.

Helen
STEWART ISLAND

Bar-tailed godwits

THE ANIMALS

Cicada (below)

Wasp (below right)

SUMMER is the insect season. Pupae change into insects. Everywhere there are insects of every shape and size – in the grasses, on plants and in trees. Mosquitoes and sandflies thrive in the summer humidity. The butterflies emerge from chrysalises and can be seen everywhere. The singing of cicadas, which hatch in the heat of summer, is a seasonal sound all over the country.

As with the birds, summertime is when the young farm and domestic animals, born in spring, fatten up on summer feed. Deer and possums, which have been introduced into this country with disastrous consequences for the native bush, are also busy raising their young in summer.

Lizards bask in the hot summer sun, while ants are busily collecting winter supplies.

Bees are gathering nectar and pollen and wasp nests are also alive with activity. As fruit ripens the wasps arrive, making fruit collecting a hazardous occupation.

Dairy farmers put the bulls out among the cows for mating.

We see one of the species of the long-horned grasshopper at our place. They are smaller than the katydid, and are hard to detect in the long grass. In the hottest time, from mid January to February, they leap about in the dozens. They surround our feet as we walk up the path.
Huhu bugs have emerged from the grub state and can give you a fright as they bash into windows at night trying to get to the light.

Shay and Bevan
PICTON

Stoats and weasels
are noticeable at
this time of year.

Rowan
NELSON

———————

We love to watch the
monarch butterflies
hatch out of their
green chrysalises.

Rachel
AUCKLAND

*Monarch butterfly
hatching from
chrysalis* (below)

THE PEOPLE

SUMMER is an active, outdoors time. People flock to the beaches and lakes to swim and fish or just laze in the warmth. Most people take their holidays in summer, when they engage in a wide range of outdoor activities, such as camping, swimming, tramping and rock climbing.

One of the greatest summertime activities is boating. Although keen boaties will be seen on the water all year round, summer sees a huge increase in water activity on the lakes and in the ocean. Every type of water craft appears, from windsurfers to canoes; from small motorised dinghies to huge luxury launches; from one-child learner yachts to the beautiful big racing yachts.

Summer is a time of predominantly small ball sports, such as cricket, softball and tennis.

The days are long and hot in summer, and it's exciting because you can stay up late.
I love the summer activities of tenting, sleeping out, caving, barbecues, bonfires on the beach.
Visitors come and everyone gets sunburnt.
The sandflies are very annoying.
The vegetables are ready: cucumbers, peas, carrots, lettuce, celery, radishes, beans and spuds.

Amiria
WESTPORT

The main shearing of sheep takes place at the beginning of the season. This is always a great undertaking on the farm, as all the sheep, including the lambs, have to be mustered and brought into the yards.

Everyone on the farm is involved in the noisy and dusty drama of shearing. If the farm is large and fairly isolated, shearing gangs who come to shear the sheep will set up camp in the shearing quarters. If there is a large mob of sheep to be shorn, the job will take some days to complete.

For those who work on the land, summer is a busy, productive time. Farmers are making hay and cropping, and fruit ripens in the summer sun. Orchardists start picking the fruit when it is ready. Gardeners are also busy tending their gardens, as garden produce is at its peak. People are busy freezing or preserving the fruit for winter.

In the summer holidays we have strange creatures come to our beach. They are very nosey, and drop lots of rubbish. They go for lots of walks and are very colourful and come in big groups. These seasonal creatures are campers.

Bethany
LEITHFIELD BEACH,
NORTH CANTERBURY

I like hay making in summer because the hay smells nice. We go swimming in the lake after. We also water ski in the lake. We take the horses across in a barge to the races at Glenorchy.

Brylee
GLENORCHY,
SOUTHLAND

AUTUMN
Ngahuru

Supplej

In autumn leaves
fall down,
Umbrellas, kites,
paper, rubbish flying
everywhere.
The tree leaves are
changing colour,
Up they rise, then
float down gently.
Mornings are now
much colder,
Now we are wearing
warmer clothes.

Rebecca
KAITAIA,
NORTHLAND

AUTUMN begins on the first day of March. The equinox falls between 20 and 23 March and the days begin to get noticeably shorter. Autumn, like spring, is an 'in-between' season or 'adolescent' season. As in spring the length of the days and nights are roughly the same.

The general weather pattern of autumn is often fairly settled. Autumn is loved and enjoyed for its (sometimes) still, calm weather, when there is no wind. When this occurs, the air is usually cold and crisp in the morning, and the day is fine and sunny.

As in spring there are, however, some equinoctial winds, particularly in the lower parts of the North Island. When they come the winds are strong, but they are not usually as persistent as the spring equinoctials. They blow the dying leaves off the deciduous trees, and spread seeds from plants and trees.

Autumn mists are quite common in the early mornings, especially in river valleys. Sometimes they can stay until quite late in the morning.

As the season progresses, frosts begin to fall, especially in the southern regions. The temperatures all over the country start to get colder, especially at night. The first frost is always well marked by people: so is the first snowfall seen on the mountain ranges.

The dews are much heavier in autumn. In most places in New Zealand there is enough humidity to bring about the damper conditions for dew. Many gardens need little watering at this time even if there has been no rain and the days are warm and sunny.

In autumn we like to make big piles of leaves and hide in them.

Jonathan
AUCKLAND

Location	Rainfall Total (mm) mean monthly	Temperature Mean daily maximum °C	Sunshine Mean hours per day	Relative Humidity Mean daily (%)
Auckland	120	20.3	5.3	81
Napier	73	19.8	5.6	75
Ruapehu	212	12.7	4.3	87
Wellington	108	16.6	5.1	83
Nelson	89	17.9	6.1	84
Christchurch	59	17.5	5.0	83
Dunedin	71	15.1	3.8	77

We like hunting for different seeds in autumn.

Rachel
AUCKLAND

THE SKY

THE SUN is beginning to wane in autumn. It is no longer too hot to sit in the sun in the hottest part of the day.

The Southern Cross and its pointers, Alpha Centauri and Beta Centauri, are seen high in the autumn evening sky. The Southern Cross is only seen in the Southern Hemisphere, and although it is a small constellation, the four main stars are very bright and easy to spot.

In autumn the leaves flutter like birds dancing, then coming down to land to look for pink worms. They look like a colourful blanket on the ground. We run through them making crunchy sounds with our feet.

Thunder, our pony, grows his furry coat ready for a tough cold winter.

In late autumn, Dad goes away on our four-wheeler motorbike to muster the sheep from our summer grazing blocks. He brings them down to the lake's edge where it doesn't get as much snow. It is a very busy time for us, because the sheep have to be crutched.

Alana
LAKE TEKAPO,
SOUTH CANTERBURY

Vega is first seen rising in the east in February, but to the Maori it was always associated with the harvest. They knew the star as Whanui.

In the earlier part of the evening, Sirius is almost overhead, as is Canopus.

The zodiacal constellations which appear in the early evening are: Virgo, Leo, Cancer, Gemini and Taurus. In the early morning Scorpius, Sagittarius and Capricornus can be seen.

At the end of summer and through autumn, we often get crystal clear skies at night and it is dead still. We call it the earthquake season.

Chris
CENTRAL HAWKE'S BAY

*Southern Cross
with its pointers*

THE waters around the coast are beginning to get cold again as the sun wanes and the days get shorter. In autumn the big snapper move closer to shore, before they withdraw from our coast for winter.

In late April-May, an annual migration of moki occurs between Kaikoura and East Cape. The fish are travelling north to their spawning grounds.

Terakihi is a late summer-autumn spawner in several areas around New Zealand, so this is the time for the commercial fishing of this species.

The female crayfish moult in autumn, and spawning occurs within a few weeks of her moult.

Early autumn sees visiting fishing boats at the wharf ferrying local Maori to their mutton-birding islands.

Helen
STEWART ISLAND

In the inland waterways, eels begin congregating at the outlets of dams and lakes, ready for their migration. This is a time when they can be easily caught with nets. A few days before a big weather depression, they can be seen in ever greater numbers, waiting for the rains to wash them out into the rivers, which they will follow out to sea. They will then travel to grounds near Samoa (the shortfin eel), or near to Tonga (the longfin eel), to spawn.

Once they have spawned, their life cycle is over. Eel larvae are then transported to New Zealand by the South Equatorial Current. They begin to enter New Zealand fresh water as baby eels (glass-eels) at the end of winter, and will carry on arriving through spring.

In autumn trout start on their journey upstream to spawn. The brown trout leave earlier than the rainbow trout, which go up in May or June. They wait for floods to travel upstream, and pair up on the way to the shallow headwaters.

Longfin eel

Around March we see the kingfish come into the Sounds and hang around the salmon farms trying to get the salmon. They are a sought-after game fish and fight strongly when hooked.

Kathy
PICTON

———

Autumn is a great time for catching trout because they are all hungry and moving upstream.

Chris
CENTRAL HAWKE'S BAY

Rainbow trout

THE LAND

We love autumn time best, when the leaves start changing. It begins with the rowans, followed by the willows, poplars and elms. The larches are last. These trees were planted by the settlers of the 1880s. The best time to see all this colour is the middle to the end of April. By the end of autumn everything has lost its leaves, except for the pines and the native beech trees.

Sally
MT ALGIDUS,
CANTERBURY

AUTUMN is harvest time on the farms, in the gardens, and in the native forests.

In the orchards, huge harvests of apples are gathered. Other autumn fruits include feijoas, tamarillos, persimmons, and many kinds of pears.

Kumaras are harvested in the North Island, particularly Northland and coastal regions where they grow well. Pumpkins, corn and all sorts of root vegetables, such as potatoes and carrots, are also harvested.

Around the vineyards the sound of bird scarers can be heard as the grapes ripen. When they are ripe enough they are picked and pressed to make wine by the vintners.

One of the most noticeable aspects of autumn is the colouring of the leaves on the deciduous trees. Almost all of these trees have been introduced from the Northern Hemisphere. The beautiful reds, oranges and yellows are a wonderful sight as the autumn progresses. Late in the season the tidy orchards can look quite spectacular with their rows and rows of orange-leafed trees.

In gardens most of the flowers are fading and dying. The last of the summer vegetables are harvested before the frosts come. A number of plants like chrysanthemums flower in autumn and brighten up the gardens which have lost their summer colour.

Wild briar roses on the roadsides are covered with small bright red rose-hips.

In autumn we have to get some matches to burn off the stubble paddocks. Daddy mows and grubs around the fence line and we start the fires.
I can spread the fire along with a pitchfork. It is very hot and the fire crackles.

Tim
TIMARU

THE NATIVE FORESTS

AUTUMN is harvest time in native forests, as it is on the farms, in gardens and in orchards. It is seed collecting time for people who want to grow native trees and plants.

The birds greatly benefit from the array of ripening berries which come in many different colours and shapes. The karaka berries are very plump by autumn and turn a beautiful bright orange. The coprosma family has berries in all sorts of colours: orange, yellow, white, red and blue.

By autumn the podocarp family all have their berries fully ripened. Totara berries ripen to bright red; the miro to purplish red; and the matai to black.

Kowhai seeds are presented in an unusual package. Like the seeds of the manuka, kanuka and flax (harakeke), they are ripe and plentiful. Rimu and kahikatea seeds are much enjoyed by the birds. The tiny black seeds lie inside a juicy red cushion.

The hot orange berries of the New Zealand passion vine (kohia) are a fantastic sight where the vine is seen climbing a tree. One tree which flowers in autumn is the lacebark (hoheria). With all the colour of berries and flowers, it can be very pleasant walking in the bush at this time of the year.

A number of fungi also appear in autumn. The staghorn fungus and ear fungus are found in the beech forests. There are also some autumn orchids, which are found in special places.

In autumn the blackberries are ripe to eat.
The fuchsia berries and the coprosma berries are also ripe for eating.
We see the white herons on the river flats after their chicks have left home.
We hear the deer roaring in their mating rituals.

Jennifer, Sam and Elinor
BARN BAY,
SOUTH WESTLAND

Coprosma berries
(right)

Karaka fruit

Lacebark flowers

In the month of
April, cockatoos fly
in groups of up to
12, screeching
loudly. This is the
only time we see
them. At this time
also, the karamu
berries are edible,
and young children
like to take whole
branches and pick off
the tiny delicacies.

Helen
NGARUAWAHIA,
WAIKATO

Kowhai seed pods

Ear fungus (left)

THE BIRDS

AUTUMN is feast time for the birds. The native birds gorge themselves on native berries. The kereru (New Zealand pigeon) can get so fat that they cannot move. They peck at their own breasts to release the fat under their skin.

Bellbirds and tuis can be watched revelling in the abundant food supply.

Autumn in New Zealand is spring-time in the Northern Hemisphere. The migratory birds which arrived here in spring are now ready to make the long journey home for breeding. But instead of the thin drab birds who arrived in spring, they are now fat and colourful.

Gulls can be seen inland gathering in large flocks. All the adult male godwits and knots (the most common of the migratory birds) have changed into their breeding dress, and are coloured a vivid red underneath. As the time comes for them to leave New Zealand, they mob up in huge flocks on the mudflats and estuaries, and leave together.

In autumn the smaller birds, such as chaffinches, silvereyes and sparrows, are seen feasting on the rose-hips off the briar bushes. Hundreds of paradise ducks flock from far and wide into the close paddocks, where there is good autumn feed, and dams. In April the frosts start.

Rowena and Grant
BLENHEIM

On the first Saturday in May the duck shooting starts. Near our beach is a lagoon which is a bird sanctuary. It is covered with birds at this time of the year.

Michael
WAIROA,
HAWKE'S BAY

Silvereyes

Ducks (left)

The birds start gathering about three days before they actually leave. Seeing them take off is a remarkable sight. The flocks can number several thousand, and people have described the sky as going quite black because there are so many birds taking off at the same time.

In the gannet colonies, all the birds start to leave in autumn. By the middle of April, there are only a few adults left. The young birds have set off on their epic journey across the Tasman Sea to Australia. It is a huge flight for the young birds, and many do not survive. They do not return for three years, when they come back to their home colony to breed.

Kakapo chicks are born in autumn (March).

In March the godwits depart
from Farewell Spit.
The wild banana passionfruit ripen.
We see the freshwater eels
go out to sea.

Rowan
GOLDEN BAY,
NELSON

———

The black teals which arrived in September and spent summer on the lagoon, leave our beach at the end of April.
The waxeyes arrive about April and entertain us with their cheerful chirping and darting.
The bellbirds come to Leithfield Beach in April or May. They come from Mt Grey because it is too cold for them in winter up there. They sip nectar with their long beaks, and make a bell-like sound.

Anna and Luke
LEITHFIELD BEACH,
SOUTH CANTERBURY

Waders mobbing to migrate

Gannet colony (right)

THE ANIMALS

THE animals prepare for winter, by moulting and regrowing thick new coats. Sheep grow their wool; deer and possums grow thicker coats. Chickens go off the lay and begin to moult.

The calves from last spring are weaned from their mothers at this time, which is a very noisy few days on the farm.

In autumn, male deer shed a part of their antlers. It is their breeding season, and they can be heard roaring in the bush where they live. This roaring is territorial.

Spiders are very noticeable in autumn, as many young ones come into houses and spin their webs. They tend to venture inside after rain.

The black cricket (puwhanga) sings a faint musical song throughout autumn. This is a sound of autumn, just as the cicada is a sound of summer.

An artificial seasonal rhythm is the migration of many ducks to 'safe' ponds and lakes in towns and cities, just before the beginning of the duck shooting season.

In autumn all the leaves fall and the grass goes brown. We do the autumn muster. Mum and Dad do it with help from other people. The helicopter picks them up really early and takes them up the hill. If they had to walk it would take four days. Dad gets the cows and calves out of the caples to wean the calves. The yards are near the house, and the cows moo all night. Weaning takes two days. I hate this time. We start to feed out. I like feeding out, but I have to do schoolwork.

Brylee
GLENORCHY,
SOUTHLAND

In autumn we are overrun with snails. We can go out at night and pick up 900 snails off the paths! We fill ice-cream containers with them and feed them to the chooks.

Kathy
PICTON

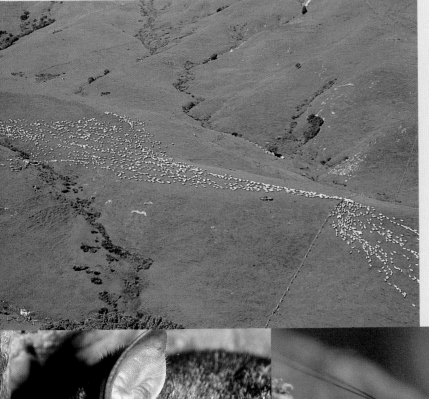

Slowly the red and
yellow leaves float
to the ground,
Light, gentle,
brittle, not making
a sound,
Forming a crunchy
carpet,
Soon the tree is
bare.
The crickets sing of
a happy day far away,
They say they are not
singing their last
song,
Here come the snow
clouds,
They are wrong!

David
WANGANUI

The autumn muster
(top)

Black cricket (above)

Possum (left)

Red deer (opposite)

In autumn the
gentians flower and
the chamois coats
turn black.

Lil
EREWHON STATION,
CANTERBURY

THE PEOPLE

In autumn it is
getting colder,
The ground is covered
in colours.
We don't go swimming
any more.
We have some apples
on our trees.

Erin and George
EKETAHUNA,
MANAWATU

———

I love autumn.
I love it when the
grapes ripen.
I love it when the
yellowhammers come to
feed on the grass
seeds.
I love it when the
corn, spuds, wheat
and apples ripen.
The days get shorter
and the weather gets
colder.
The leaves fall off
some trees, but not
our native trees.
I feel happy because
food is ready, but it
makes me sad because
it is closer to
winter and I can't
play outside as long.
I have to wear warmer
clothes because it is
colder.

Tineke
WESTPORT

AUTUMN affects people in different ways. When the weather is settled, the still, crisp days are very enjoyable.

People who work on the land are very busy with their harvests. Many crops would be damaged by frost and cold weather, so they must be gathered in time.

In the commercial gardens, machines and people are harvesting the autumn crops such as apples, potatoes, tomatoes, corn and pumpkins. The big combine-harvesters are out working long hours in the paddocks harvesting the grain crops such as wheat, barley and oats.

'He huanga ki matiti, he tama ki tokerau' (A relative in summer, a son in autumn) is a humourous Maori proverb for the season. In summer when there is work to be done, he claims to be only a distant relative, but in autumn at harvest time, he claims to be a son.

Mushroom-gathering and picking blackberries are favourite autumn pastimes. The mushrooms pop up overnight in grassy places like paddocks and people collect them in the mornings. Blackberries grow wild on prickly vines.

Everyone prepares themselves for winter. This may mean stocking up the woodpile, or getting some new warm clothes – whatever might be needed to get ready for the cold weather to come.

We love picking blackberries down on the river bank in autumn. We eat lots of blackberries while we are picking. Mum makes blackberry and apple pie.

Ben
CENTRAL HAWKE'S BAY

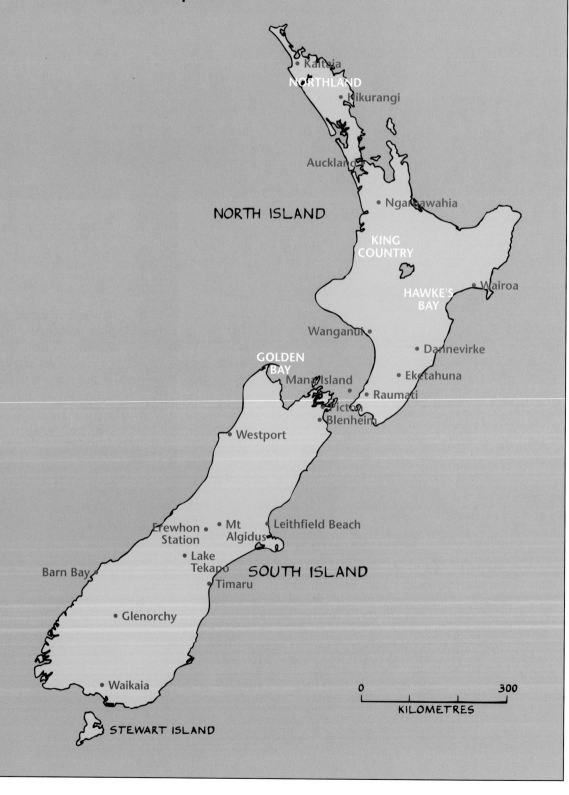

Location of children who contributed quotes

Kaitaia

NORTHLAND

Kikurangi

Auckland

NORTH ISLAND

Ngaruawahia

KING COUNTRY

HAWKE'S BAY

Wairoa

Wanganui

GOLDEN BAY

Dannevirke

Mana Island

Eketahuna

Picton

Raumati

Blenheim

Westport

Erewhon Station

Mt Algidus

Leithfield Beach

Lake Tekapo

SOUTH ISLAND

Barn Bay

Timaru

Glenorchy

Waikaia

STEWART ISLAND

0   300

KILOMETRES

INDEX